"LOVE IS THE REASON FOR LIFE"
—Susan Polis Schutz

SUSAN WILL TOUCH YOU,
AWAKEN YOU,
FILL YOUR HEART WITH LOVE!

"A poet of the heart."
—*Family Weekly*

❤

"In high emotion...the reigning star is Susan Polis Schutz."
—*Time*

❤

"Susan Polis Schutz remains one of the most popular poets in America today, and her work touches virtually everyone."
—**Associated Press**

❤

"My own favorite words of love are by a young nationally known poet, Susan Polis Schutz, and her husband, Stephen Schutz. It is a collaborative effort of her words and his art. She talks of real love as meaning 'sharing' rather than 'controlling' each other's lives."
—**Letitia Baldridge, syndicated columnist**
Los Angeles Times

❤

"Susan Polis Schutz's popularity can be attributed to her ability to verbalize intimate, honest emotions shared but unsaid by most people. Her ability to write simply and honestly of the deepest emotions and the most fragile and fleeting of moments strikes a responsive chord with readers."
—*Woman's Day*

❤

"Susan Polis Schutz and Stephen Schutz's work initiates love affairs, confirms people's love for each other, reminds us of the beauty of nature—and you need not be a romantic to see their magic. Susan is America's most published poet and author of today's most often exchanged love poems."
—*New England Bride*

SUSAN POLIS SCHUTZ IS THE WINNER OF THE FIRST ROMANTIC POET AWARD FROM THE *ROMANTIC TIMES*.

Other books by
Susan Polis Schutz

Come Into the Mountains, Dear Friend

I Want to Laugh, I Want to Cry

Peace Flows from the Sky

Someone Else to Love

Yours if You Ask

Love, Live & Share

Find Happiness in Everything You Do

Don't Be Afraid to Love

Take Charge of Your Body
by Susan Polis Shutz and Katherine F. Carson, M.D.

To My Daughter with Love
on the Important Things in Life

To My Son with Love

Mother, I Will Always Love You

I Love You

Susan Polis Schutz

Designed and illustrated by

Stephen Schutz

(originally published as *Love*)

WARNER BOOKS

A Time Warner Company

Warner Books Edition

Warner Books, Inc., 666 Fifth Avenue, New York, NY 10103

A Time Warner Company

Printed in the United States of America

First Warner Books Printing: February 1991
10 9 8 7 6 5 4 3

Library of Congress Cataloging-in-Publication Data

Schutz. Susan Polis.
    [Love]
    I love you /Susan Polis Schutz ; designed and illustrated by Stephen Schutz.
        p. cm.
    Originally published: Love. Boulder, Colo.: Blue Mountain Press, c1989.
    ISBN 0-446-39144-1
    1. Love poetry. American. I. Schutz, Stephen. II. Tltle.
PS3569.C556L6   1991
811'.54—dc20
                                            90-46824
                                                CIP

CONTENTS

Introduction
I love you
With you I can be myself
In the past, love was only a dream
Thank you for the day we met
    and I love you
I love you for being so honest
I love you so much
Love
I want to walk with you in love
When we first met I held back so much
Before I met you
Love takes time
I will stay in love with you . . .
Sometimes I am in a room full of people
Sometimes I wake up
Love can last forever if you want it to
Expressing hurt feelings may be hard,
    but it is important
Always be honest in love
Though I may not have shown it lately,
    I am so thankful for our beautiful love
I look at your face
No matter what, I love you
The importance of love
Feelings are important
You are my world, you are my love
Without love, I could not enjoy life
I am always here
Only love can assure us that the world
    will remain beautiful
All the moments of love
I miss you so

48 I never knew how it felt
49 In the morning
51 No one is perfect
52 Take risks for love
53 Don't be afraid to love
55 Many experiences and feelings may be
        necessary before being ready to love
56 Music touches feelings
57 When I wake up and see you
        in the morning
58 My body is on fire with the
        afterglow of love
59 I want to wake him
60 Make a triumph of every aspect of life
61 Always appreciate the person you love
62 Everyone needs reassurance
        that they are loved
63 Don't take love for granted
64 Treat each day as if love were new
65 It is sad when people are not willing
        to work at love
66 You must be happy with yourself before
        someone else can be happy with you
67 It is not necessary to follow
        preconceived ideas
69 I want to have a lasting relationship
        with you, even though it
        may not always be easy
70 Love is . . .
72 I want our relationship to last
75 I love you more than "love"
77 My dream is you
78 About the Authors

I Love You

*I can't say I love you enough
because it is the most
beautiful, complete feeling
I have ever had
Over and over again
I love you*

—Susan Polis Schutz

INTRODUCTION

Love is the strongest, most complete and fulfilling emotion possible. Shortly after I met Stephen Schutz in Princeton, New Jersey, I knew that I was in love with him. And now I still remain even more deeply in love with him than ever.

I LOVE YOU is written to Stephen as an expression of my feelings for him, and as a way to thank him for our beautiful relationship.

> "Not only did you
> bring back my
> belief in dreams
> but you are even
> more wonderful
> than my dreams"

Susan Polis Schutz

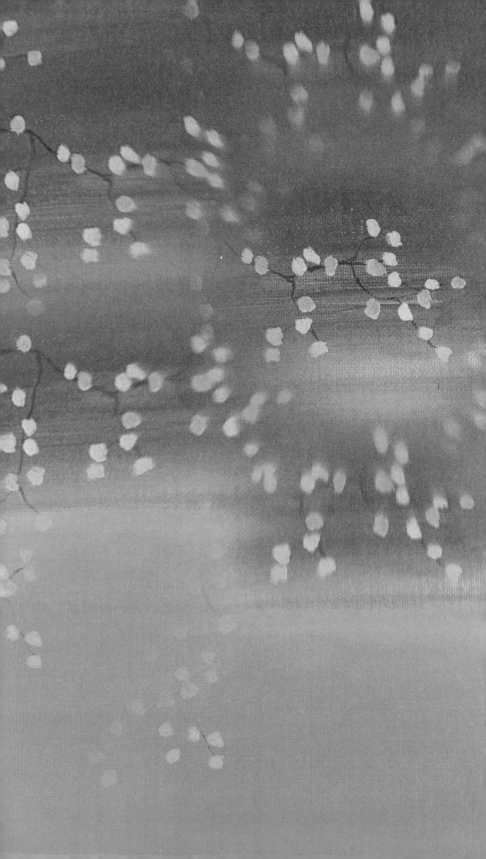

I love you

I
cannot promise you that
I will not change
I cannot promise you that
I will not have many different moods
I cannot promise you that
I will not hurt your feelings sometimes
I cannot promise you that
I will not be erratic
I cannot promise you that
I will always be strong
I cannot promise you that
my faults will not show
But —
I do promise you that
I will always be supportive of you
I do promise you that
I will share all my thoughts
*   and feelings with you*
I do promise you that
I will give you freedom to be yourself
I do promise you that
I will understand everything that you do
I do promise you that
I will be completely honest with you
I do promise you that
I will laugh and cry with you
I do promise you that
I will help you achieve all your goals
But —
most of all
I do promise you that
I love you

*W*ith you
I can be myself
and I do not have to
pretend to be
anything that I am not
With you
I can say and think everything
I want to
and I know that I will be understood
With you
I can be totally free
in body and mind
and I can share my
deepest feelings and emotions
With you
I am filled with a love
that gives me strength and happiness
And I want to thank you for this
and make sure that
you know that
I love you

In the past, love was only a dream

I always thought that
our kind of relationship
only existed in dreams —

In the past
I did not want to let anyone really know me
Now
I find that I am telling you things
that I long ago forgot
because I want you to understand
*   everything about me*

In the past
I only wanted people to see the best of me
Now
I find that I do not mind if you see my faults
because I want you to accept me the way I am

In the past
I thought that only I could make the
right decisions for myself
Now
I can discuss all my ideas with you
and you can help me make decisions
because I have such a complete trust in you . . .

In the past
I didn't care how I treated people
Now
I find that I have a new sensitivity
    towards everyone
because my softest emotions
    have been awakened by you

In the past
love was a word that I was not sure of
Now
I find that inside of me
every fiber, every nerve, every emotion
    every feeling
is exploding
in an overwhelming emotion of love
and that love is all for you

I always thought that
our kind of relationship
only existed in dreams —

Now
I have found out that
our kind of relationship
is even better than my dreams
I love you

Thank you for the day we met and I love you

Ever since the day we met
I knew that you were extremely special
I knew that I wanted to get to know you better
and I knew that my emotions had been touched
Ever since the day I fell in love with you
I knew that I wanted to spend all my time with you
I knew that I wanted to tell you everything about myself
I knew that I would begin to grow as a person
Ever since the day that you and I became one
I knew that we had a very poignant relationship
I knew that my body and mind were passionate forever
I knew that I wanted our relationship to last forever
If we had not met
I would still be searching for happiness
and I would always be thinking that love was not real
So I want to dearly thank you
for the day we met and
I love you

*I love you
for being so honest
for being so free
for being so trusting
for being so passionate
and for contributing so much
to our relationship*

*I love you
for all you do for me
for all you express to me
for all you share with me
and for all that you are*

*I love you
for understanding me
for laughing and crying
with me
for having fun with me
and for being such
an outstanding person*

*I love you
for being so strong
for being so independent
for being so creative
and for being such a unique person*

*I love you
for all these things and more
I love you
for everything about you*

I love you

I love you so much

Since I met you
I have been so happy
except that I find
myself worrying all the time —
worrying that I might disappoint you
worrying that our relationship might end
worrying that you might not be happy
worrying that something might happen to you
I have fallen in love with you
and I guess I worry so much
because I care about you so much

Love

*L*ove is
the strongest feeling known
an all-encompassing passion
an extreme strength
an overwhelming excitement

Love is
trying not to hurt
   the other person
trying not to change
   the other person
trying not to dominate
   the other person
trying not to deceive
   the other person

Love is
understanding each other
listening to each other
supporting each other
having fun with each other...

Love is
not an excuse to stop growing
not an excuse to stop making yourself better
not an excuse to lessen one's goals
not an excuse to take the
other person for granted

Love is
being completely honest with each other
finding dreams to share
working towards common goals
sharing responsibilities equally

Everyone in the world wants to love
Love is not a feeling
to be taken lightly
Love is a feeling to be cherished
nurtured and cared for
Love is
the reason for life

I want to walk with you in love
I want to talk to you
 about what I cannot say to others
I want to laugh with you
 even when I feel silly
I want to cry with you
 when you are most upset
I want to plan with you
 all my dreams
I want to share with you
 all the beautiful things in life
I want to fight with you
 against all the ugly things in life
I want to create with you
 dreams to follow
I want to have fun with you
 in whatever we do
I want to work with you
 towards common goals
I want to dance with you
 to the rhythm of our love
I love you

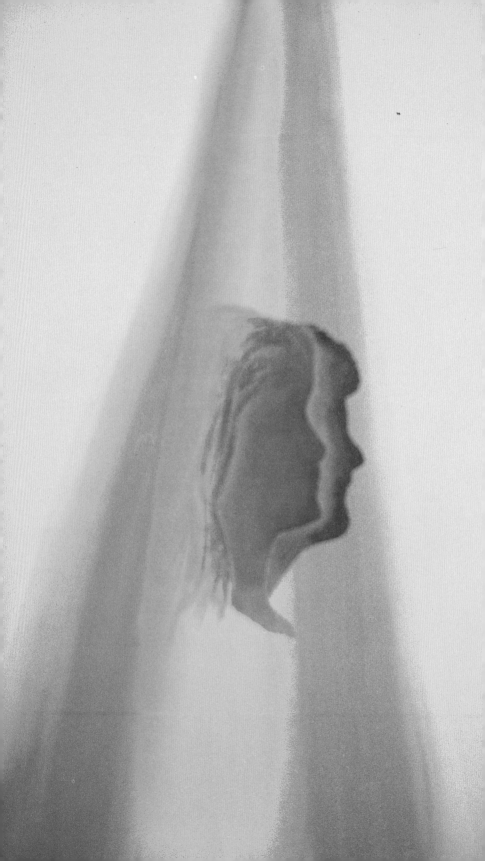

When we first met
I held back so much
afraid to show my deepest feelings
As I got to know you better
your gentleness and honesty
encouraged me to open up
and I started a trust
in you that I never had
with anyone else
Once I started to express
my feelings
I realized that
this is the only way
to have a relationship
It is such a
wonderful feeling
to let myself
be completely known to you
Thank you
so much
for showing me
what two people can
share together
I love you

Before I met you
I was a robot
who went to work
at certain times
who played
at certain times
who laughed
at certain times
and who cried
at certain times
You awoke feelings
inside of me
that I never knew existed
As we started to get
closer and closer
you broke through the
machine of me
and discovered the
human being of me
You made my life
complete

Love takes time

Please be gentle
with my feelings
It will take time
because I have
been hurt
Please be gentle
with your words
It will take time
because I have heard
too many lies
Please be gentle
with your eyes
It will take time
because I have seen
too many deceitful looks
Please be gentle
with your body
It will take time
because I have felt
too many cold bodies
Please be gentle
with your love
There is a beauty
in being gentle
that only real love
can understand

I will stay in love with you...

*H*ow can I stay in love
with you forever?
How can we make our relationship into
a lifetime of sharing and joy?

In order to stay in love forever
I must first find the right person to love
and I have, in you

In order to stay in love forever
we both must understand each other and ourselves
and we must be completely honest
    with each other at all times
We both must have our own goals and interests
and actively pursue them
We both must have complete freedom of thought
and we must encourage each other
    to follow our dreams . . .

In order to stay in love forever
we must always be fair, kind and supportive
   of each other
We must dedicate ourselves to being
   equal partners in all that we feel
   and in all that we do
We must promise each other that
   we will always create time
   to just appreciate each other and our love
and that we will never be lazy
   and take our love for granted

In order for me to stay in love
with you forever
and have a relationship that is
a lifetime of sharing and loving
I must really pledge myself
   to this wonderful commitment
and I must really want to stay in love
with you forever
and I do

*S*ometimes I am
in a room full of people
and our eyes meet
and I feel so comfortable

Sometimes I am
afraid to do something
and our eyes meet
and I feel so confident

Sometimes I
don't know if I have
made the right decision
and our eyes meet
and I feel so reassured

Sometimes I am
very confused
and our eyes meet
and I know I am understood

When our eyes meet
the love that we have for each other
shines through
giving me such strength and happiness
When our eyes meet
our hearts unite
and your love
creates a protective rainbow over me
and the world becomes
   a peaceful garden
I love you

Sometimes I wake up
in the middle of the night
shivering from fright
feeling empty
feeling nothing
because I think about
how it would be
if you weren't here
And then I wonder
if you really know
how very much
you mean to me
how incredible
I think you are
how you are
a part of all my emotions
how you are
the deepest meaning in my life
Please always know
that I love you
more than anything else
in the world

Love can last forever if you want it to

*L*ove is the strongest and
most fulfilling emotion possible
It lets you share
your goals, your desires, your experiences
It lets you share
your life with someone
It lets you be yourself
  with someone who will always support you
It lets you speak
your innermost feelings
  to someone who understands you
It lets you feel tenderness and warmth —
  a wholeness that avoids loneliness
Love lets you feel complete

But in order to have
a lasting love relationship
you must make a strong commitment to each other and love
and you must do and feel everything within your mind and be
  to make this commitment work

You must be happy with yourself
  and you must understand yourself
before you can expect someone else
to be happy with you or to understand you
You must be honest about yourself and each other at all times
  and not hold any feelings back
You must accept each other the way you are
  and not try to change each other
You must be free to grow as individuals yet share your life as
  but not live your life through each other
You must follow your own principles and morals
  and not follow what societal roles tell you to do
You must follow the philosophy that men and women are equa
  and not treat either person with inferiority in any way . . .

In order to have
a lasting love relationship
you must be together always in your heart
    but not necessarily always in your activities
You must be proud of each other and love
    and not be ashamed to show your sensitive feelings
You must treat every day spent with each other as special
    and not take each other or your love for granted
You must spend time talking with each other every day
    and not be too busy with outside events that you
    are too tired for each other
You must understand each other's moods and feelings
    and not hurt each other intentionally
    but if your frustrations are taken out on each other
    you must both realize that it is not a personal attack
You must be passionate with each other often
    and not get into boring patterns
You must continue to have fun and excitement with each other
    and not be afraid to try new things
You must always work at love and your love relationship
    and not forget how important this relationship is or what
    you would feel like without it

Love is the strongest
and most fulfilling emotion possible
If you commit yourself to love
love can last forever if you want it to
and I do

ressing hurt feelings
may be hard, but it is
important

Sometimes it may not seem
that I love you
Sometimes it may not seem
that I even like you
It is at these times
that you really need to
understand me more than ever
because it is at these times
that I love you more than ever
but my feelings have been hurt
Even though I try not to
I know that I am acting cold
   and indifferent
It is at these times that I find it so hard
to express my feelings
Often what you have done to
hurt my feelings is so small
but when you love someone
like I love you
small things become big things
and the first thing I think about
is that you do not love me
Please be patient with me
I am trying to be more honest
with my feelings
and I am trying not to be so sensitive
but in the meantime
I think you should be very confident that
at all times
in every way possible
I love you

*Always be honest
in love*

*B*ecause
our relationship
is based on
honesty and
fairness
there is no
need to test
each other
It is so
wonderful
to find someone
whom I
don't need
to play games
with
and who lives
up to everything that
I consider
important, right and
beautiful

Though I may not have shown it lately, I am so thankful for our beautiful love

I know that I have
been preoccupied with
everything that is going on
I have been looking
right through you lately
until today
when I noticed
a hurt look in your eyes
a look of loneliness
I am so sorry
The outside events
in my life
are not nearly as important
as what is inside my life—
you
and my love for you
I am so glad
that I looked
into your eyes
They jolted sense
back into me
My tears
are from
happiness and
thankfulness
for the
beautiful
love
we share
You will never
be lonely again
My love for you
will warm you
forever

I look at your face
It is so strong
I look at your eyes
They are so soft
I hear you speak
Your words are so wise
I watch your actions
You are such an individualist
I talk to you
You understand the meaning behind
   whatever I say
You are everything
that is beautiful
I am so lucky
to have met you
and I want to
tell you
over and over again that
I have fallen in love with you
and the more
I learn about you
the more
I love you

*No matter what,
I love you*

*I often wonder what
made us fall in love
with each other
We are so different
from each other
Our strengths and weaknesses
are so different
Our ways of approaching things
are so different
Our personalities
are so different
Yet our love
continues to grow and grow
Perhaps the differences we have
add to the excitement of our relationship
We are basically different from
each other
but we have so many
feelings and emotions in common
And it really doesn't matter
why we fell
in love
All that matters to me
is that we continue
to respect and love
each other*

The importance of love

Love is so important
We can have all the possessions in the world
but if we don't have someone to love
we have nothing at all
Love makes our emotions complete

Love is so important
It brings out the best in each of us
We learn from each other's lives
and grow from our differences
We are two individuals
living our own lives
with each other as one
Love enlightens us

Love is so important
As a couple in love
we are stronger, more sensitive
more aware, more knowing
and more at peace
than we are individually
Love makes us better people

Love is so important
It gives understanding to all that we do
because we are able to share our ideas
explain our goals
express our frustrations
and always have someone to support
what we say and do
Love makes it a lot easier
to achieve what we want in life

Feelings are important

I always thought that
what I do each day
is so vital
what I say each day
is so necessary
what I learn each day
is so stimulating
but I have found out that
what I feel each day
is the most gratifying
and my love for you
is the deepest feeling I have
Thank you for your love
It is the most important and
beautiful part of my life
I love you

You are my world,
you are my love

What if we had never met?
What would I be doing?
What kind of life would I have?
I often think about these things
and I always come to the same conclusion —
without you
I would be an extremely unhappy person
living an unhappy life
I know that we met for a reason
and that reason was that
you and I were meant to be
in love with each other
You and I were meant to be
a team giving us strength
to function happily in the world
I am so thankful that things
turned out the way they did
and we were brought together
You are my world
You are my love

Without love,
I could not enjoy life

I don't know what I would do
if I didn't have you
How could I survive the daily pressures
if I didn't have you
to discuss them with
How could I survive the injustices I encounter
if I didn't have you
to give me strength
How could I survive the confusing words of others
if I didn't have you
to help me sort the words out
How could I survive all the things I want to do
if I didn't have you
to support me
How could I enjoy the beauty
of life
of touching nature
of feeling complete
of looking forward to every new minute
of understanding the joy of being one
    with another person
of a love that envelops my entire being
transforming me into
the mountains
the oceans
the flowers
the sun
I could not survive
I could not enjoy life
without you
and your love

I am always here
to understand you
I am always here
to laugh with you
I am always here
to cry with you
I am always here
to talk to you
I am always here
to think with you
I am always here
to plan with you
Even though we
might not always
be together
please know that
I am always
here to
love
you

Only love can assure us that the world will remain beautiful

I look around
and I see
the blossoming trees
I see
pink sunsets
I see
children skipping and laughing
I look around
and I also see
people discussing nuclear war
and I wonder how we
could have made such destructive forces
in such a beautiful world
I look around
and there are so many
frightening things
But then I see you
and I know that
my love for you
gives me the will
to appreciate the good things in life
and the strength to
fight against the bad
I see you
and I know
that only love
can assure us
that the world
will remain beautiful
Thank you
for making my own world
beautiful

*all the moments
of love*

I love the moments
we spend together
just being silent
I love the moments
we spend together
just being with friends
              or relatives
I love the moments
we spend together
just talking
I love the moments
we spend together
just dreaming
I love the moments
we spend together
expressing our love

I miss you so

*T*hough you are not here
wherever I go
or whatever I do
I see your face in my mind
   and I miss you so
I miss telling you everything
I miss showing you things
I miss our eyes
secretly giving each other confidence
I miss your touch
I miss our excitement together
I miss everything we share
I don't like missing you
It is a very cold and lonely feeling
I wish that I could be
with you right now
where the warmth of our love
would melt the winter snows
But since I cannot be
with you right now
I will have to be content
just dreaming about
when we will be together again

I never knew how it felt
to be alone
until you went away

so alone

I tried doing the things
we did together
but they only reminded me of you
I tried doing the things
we did not do together
but I couldn't get involved
in anything
I tried smiling
but tears were always in my eyes
I tried laughing
but nothing was funny

so alone

I never knew how it felt
to be alone
until you went away
I never knew how it felt
to love
until you came back

In the morning
when the sun
is just starting to light the day
I am awakened
and my first thoughts
are of you—
I love you

At night
I stare at the dark trees
silhouetted against the quiet stars
I am entranced
into a complete peacefulness
and my last thoughts are of you—
I love you

No one is perfect

Things aren't always
perfect between us
but everything
worth anything
has flaws
in it
No one is perfect
therefore no
relationship can be perfect
Often by seeing
the dry brown petals
in a rose
you appreciate more
the vivid red petals
that are so beautiful
And I do appreciate
our very special relationship
which is so important to me
As we continue
to grow
as individuals
our relationship
will continue to grow
more beautiful
every day

Take risks for love

S ome people laugh at love
They laugh at marriage
They laugh at happiness

It is because they have had
bad experiences that deeply hurt them
They are cynical now, doubting
anything in life that is beautiful

Don't listen to these people
Love is essential to a happy life
So take risks
Love with all your heart
Love with all your mind
It will be more than worthwhile

Don't be afraid
to love someone
totally and completely
Love is the most fulfilling
and beautiful feeling in the world
Don't be afraid that you will
get hurt
or that the other person
won't love you
There is a risk in
everything you do
and the rewards
are never so great
as what love can bring
So let yourself get involved
completely and honestly
and enjoy the possibility
that what happens
might be the only real
source of happiness

*Many experiences be
and feelings may be
necessary before being ready
to love*

I love you
Sometimes it takes adverse conditions
for people to reach out to one another
Sometimes it takes bad luck
for people to understand their goals better
Sometimes it takes a storm
for people to appreciate the calm
Sometimes it takes being hurt
for people to be more sensitive to feelings
Sometimes it takes doubt
for people to trust one another
Sometimes it takes seclusion
for people to find out who they really are
Sometimes it takes disillusionment
for people to become informed
Sometimes it takes feeling nothing
for people to feel everything
Sometimes it takes our emotions and feelings
to be completely penetrated
for people to open up to love
I have gone through many of these things
and I now know that
not only am I ready to love you
but I do

Music touches feelings
that words cannot
It is the melody
of the heart
the voice
of the spirit

Some music
causes me to dream
Some music
inspires me to create
Some music
causes me to think of the past
Some music
helps me plan the future

When I am with you
all music
moves me to love

When I wake up
and see you in the morning
I am so happy
that we are together
that we are sharing
our lives with one another
I respect you
I admire you
I love you deeply
When I wake up
each morning
and see you next to me
no matter what happens
I know that my
day will
be
all right

My body is on fire
with the afterglow of love
Thunder and lightning and earthquakes
can't equal my passion with you

My heart is on fire
with the emotions of our love
Blue skies and rainbows and flowers
can't equal my enchantment with you

I want to wake him
and say thank you
thank you for
knowing me

I want to wake him
and say thank you
thank you for
understanding me

I want to wake him
and say thank you
thank you for
making me so happy

I want to wake him
and say thank you
thank you for transforming me
into erotic delirium

But there he sleeps
so quiet and peaceful
I'll just kiss him softly
and thank him tomorrow

Make a triumph of every aspect of life

*P*eople will get only what they seek
Choose your goals carefully
Know what you like
and what you do not like
Be critical about what you can do well
and what you cannot do well
Choose a career or lifestyle that interests you
and work hard to make it a success
but also have fun in what you do
Be honest with people and help them if you can
but don't depend on anyone to make life easy
or happy for you (only you can do that for yourself)
Be strong and decisive
but remain sensitive
Regard your family, and the idea of a family
as the basis for security, support and love

Understand who you are
and what you want in life
before sharing your life with someone
When you are ready to enter a relationship
make sure that the person is worthy of
everything you are physically and mentally

Strive to achieve all that you want
Find happiness in everything you do
Love with your entire being
Love with an uninhibited soul
Make a triumph
of every aspect
of your life

*Always appreciate the
person you love*

*S*ometimes
*I worry about you
You don't relax enough
You work so hard
There is so much for you to do*

*Sometimes
I worry about you
You don't realize how much you are appreciated
or how much you give of yourself to others
or what a wonderful husband you are to me*

*Other times
I am thankful
for the way you are
as I realize it is the
only way you could be*

*But at all times
I want you to know
that I love you so deeply
I respect you so greatly
and I thank you for
being the best man in the world
in every way*

*Everyone needs reassurance
that they are loved*

*Once in a while
everyone needs
to know that they
are wanted
that they are important
that they are loved
I just wanted
to tell you
that if you
ever feel this need
I would like
to be the one
to reassure you
that you are wanted
that you are important
and that I love you*

*Whenever I make
an important decision
I try to discuss it with you
Whenever I have a difficult day
I seem to forget about it
    by spending time with you
Whenever I have doubts about
    what I am doing
I can always depend on encouragement
    from you
Whenever something special happens
    to me
your happy reaction makes it
    that much better
Whenever I have new dreams
I can depend on support from you
Whenever I find myself chasing after
    the wrong things
a hug from you sets me on the right course
because I realize that the most important
thing in life
is your love
and I am so fortunate to have you
I thank you
and I love you*

*Treat each day as if
love were new*

I
 look at some couples
who seem to have
lost that spark in their eyes
and I know that can never
    happen to us
because we have such a deep
    and meaningful relationship
one that is exciting and
    fulfilling in every way
And because I never want us to
    take each other for granted
    I want to treat each day as if
    we were new to each other
I know how hard it is to find
    a relationship like ours
and I thank you every day
    and every minute
for being such a beautiful part
of my life

It is sad when people are not willing to work at love

I feel so lucky to be
in this relationship with you
Often I feel sad for people who
cannot find someone to share
  themselves with
or who are not willing to work at
keeping their relationship thriving
Thank you for being so much to me
Thank you for blending your emotions
  with mine
I truthfully cannot bear to live
  without you
I love you so deeply

You must be happy with yourself before someone else can be happy with you

*I*t takes two people
who are self-confident
and honest
to be able to care about each other
and to trust each other

It takes two people
who know themselves
and know what they want in life
to be able to share with each other
and to understand each other

It takes two people
who have strong goals
and active interests
to be able to join another person's life
and to really be one with that person

There are no two people
better suited for each other than
you and me
to be able to love each other
and to be friends forever

It is not necessary to follow preconceived ideas

One of the reasons
that we have such a
successful relationship
is that neither of us
have preconceived ideas
of what a man or woman
should or should not do
We do not adhere to
what society says our
roles should be
We each do what we do best
and equally share our responsibilities
We appreciate so much
being completely free
to make our own choices
about everything we do
We both feel that
this is the only way
to live
and the only way
to be in a successful
relationship

ant to have a lasting relationship with you, even though it may not always be easy

*I want to have a lasting relationship
with you
I know that this will mean that
we both must work hard*
>>to please each other
>>to help each other
>>to be fair and honest with each other
>>to accept each other as we really are
we both must work hard
>>to keep our individuality
>>yet also become one with each other
>>to remain strong and supportive of each other
>>in adverse times as well as good times
>>to be exciting and interesting
>>to ourselves and to each other
we both must work hard
>>to always consider each other
>>the most important person in the world
>>to always consider love
>>the most important emotion that we can feel
>>to always consider our relationship
>>the most serious and significant
>>>union of two people

*Even though it may not always be easy
to have a lasting relationship
working hard is very easy when the results can be
the beauty of a loving and lasting
us*

Love is ...

*Love is
being happy for the other person
    when they are happy
being sad for the person when they are sad
being together in good times
and being together in bad times
Love is the source of strength*

*Love is
being honest with yourself at all times
being honest with the other person at all times
telling, listening, respecting the truth
and never pretending
Love is the source of reality*

*Love is
an understanding that is so complete that
you feel as if you are a part of the other person
accepting the other person just the way they are
and not trying to change them to be something else
Love is the source of unity*

*Love is
the freedom to pursue your own desires
while sharing your experiences with the other person
the growth of one individual alongside of
and together with the growth of another individual
Love is the source of success...*

Love is
  the excitement of planning things together
  the excitement of doing things together
Love is the source of the future

Love is
  the fury of the storm
  the calm in the rainbow
Love is the source of passion

Love is
  giving and taking in a daily situation
  being patient with each other's needs and desires
Love is the source of sharing

Love is
  knowing that the other person
  will always be with you regardless of what happens
  missing the other person when they are away
  but remaining near in heart at all times
Love is the source of security

Love is the
  source of life

I want our relationship to last

I thought I would never
find the right person to love
until I met you
And since I have
always thought that
love is the most
important part of my life
I want our love to last and
to be as beautiful
as it is now
I want our love
to be the backbone
of our lives forever

Our love came naturally
but I know that
we must both work
at making it last
so I will try my hardest
at all times
to be fair and honest with you
I will strive for my own goals
and help you achieve yours . . .

I will always try
to understand you
I will always
let you know what I am thinking
I will always
try to support you
I will try
to successfully blend
our lives together
with enough freedom
to grow as individuals
I will always
consider each day
with you special
Regardless of
what events
occur in our lives
I will make
sure that our
relationship flourishes
as I will always
love and respect
you

I love you more than "love"

It is impossible to capture in words
the feelings I have for you
They are the strongest feelings that I
have ever had about anything
yet when I try to tell you them
or try to write them to you
the words do not even begin to touch
the depths of my feelings
And though I cannot explain the essence of
these phenomenal feelings
I can tell you what I feel like when I am with you
When I am with you it is as if
    I were a bird flying freely in the clear blue sky
When I am with you it is as if
    I were a flower opening up my petals of life
When I am with you it is as if
    I were the waves of the ocean crashing strongly
        against the shore
When I am with you it is as if
    I were the rainbow after the storm
        proudly showing my colors
When I am with you it is as if
    everything that is beautiful surrounds us
This is just a very small part of how wonderful I feel
    when I am with you
Maybe the word "love" was invented to explain
the deep, all-encompassing feelings that I have for you
but somehow it is not strong enough
But since it is the best word that there is
let me tell you a thousand times that
I love you more than
"love"

My dream is you

In my dreams
I pictured a person
who was
good-looking, intelligent
sensitive, talented
creative, fun
strong and wise
who would completely
overwhelm me
with love
Since dreams
can be just wishful thinking
I did not really expect
to find one person
who had all these
outstanding qualities
But then —
I met you
and not only did you
bring back my
belief in dreams
but you are even
more wonderful
than my dreams
and I love you

ABOUT THE AUTHORS

Susan began her writing career at the age of seven, producing a neighborhood newspaper for her friends in the small country town of Peekskill, New York, where she was raised. Upon entering her teen years, she began writing poetry as a means of understanding her feelings. For Susan, writing down what she was thinking and feeling brought clarity and understanding to her life, and today she heartily recommends this to everyone. She continued her writing as she attended and graduated from Rider College, where she majored in English and biology. She then entered a graduate program in physiology, while at the same time teaching elementary school in Harlem and contributing freelance articles to newspapers and magazines.

Stephen Schutz, a native New Yorker, spent his early years studying drawing and lettering as a student at the High School of Music and Art in New York City. He went on to attend M.I.T., where he received his undergraduate degree in physics. During this time, he continued to pursue his great interest in art by taking classes at the Boston Museum of Fine Arts. He then entered Princeton University, where he earned his doctoral degree in theoretical physics.

It was in 1965, at a social event at Princeton, that Susan and Stephen met, and their love affair began. Together, they participated in peace movements and anti-war demonstrations to voice their strong feelings against war and destruction of any kind. They motorcycled around the farmlands of New Jersey and spent many hours outdoors with each other, enjoying their deep love and appreciation of nature. They daydreamed of how life should be.

Susan and Stephen were married in 1969 and moved to Colorado to begin life together in the mountains, where Susan did freelance writing at home and Stephen researched solar energy in a laboratory. On the weekends, they began experimenting with printing Susan's poems, surrounded by Stephen's art, on posters that they silk-screened in their basement. They loved being together so much that it did not take long for them to begin disliking the 9-to-5 weekday separation that had resulted from their pursuing different careers. They soon decided that their being together, not just on weekends but all of the time, was more important than anything else, so Stephen left his research position in the laboratory. They packed their pickup-truck camper with the silk-screened posters they had made, and they began a year of travelling together in the camper, selling their posters in towns and cities across the country. Their love of life and for one another, which they so warmly communicate, touched the public. People wanted more of Susan's deep thoughts on life, love, family, friendship, and nature presented with the distinctive, sensitive drawings by Stephen.

And so, in 1972, in response to incredible public demand, their first book, COME INTO THE MOUNTAINS, DEAR FRIEND, was published, and history was made in the process. Today, after twenty years of marriage and spending all of their time together, Susan and Stephen continue to share their love with all of us.

I LOVE YOU is Susan's eleventh book of poetry. It follows her recent bestsellers, TO MY SON WITH LOVE and TO MY DAUGHTER, WITH LOVE, ON THE IMPORTANT THINGS IN LIFE. Her other books include: COME INTO THE MOUNTAINS, DEAR FRIEND; I WANT TO LAUGH, I WANT TO CRY; PEACE FLOWS FROM THE SKY; SOMEONE ELSE TO LOVE; YOURS IF YOU ASK; LOVE, LIVE AND SHARE; FIND HAPPINESS IN EVERYTHING YOU DO; and DON'T BE AFRAID TO LOVE. In addition to her books, Susan's poems have been published on over 200 million greeting cards and have appeared in numerous national and international magazines and high school and college textbooks. She has edited books by other well-known authors and has coauthored a women's health book entitled TAKE CHARGE OF YOUR BODY. Susan continues to work on her autobiography and also writes music. She is currently recording her poems on cassettes to the accompaniment of music which Susan has written.

In addition to designing and illustrating all of Susan's books, Stephen's art complements the words of many other well-known authors. He creates beautiful greeting cards and calendars, which feature his special airbrush and watercolor blends, his beautiful oil paintings, and his unique calligraphy. Stephen is an accomplished photographer and continues to study physics as a hobby. Together, he and Susan participate in many outdoor sports, such as hiking in the mountains, swimming in the ocean, and cross-country skiing along the Continental Divide.

Susan and Stephen have three children. They spend all of their time with their family, including their children in everything that they do. Half of their time is spent travelling, and the other half is spent working together in their studio in Colorado. Theirs is an atmosphere of joy, love, and spontaneous creativity as they continue to produce the words, the poems, the rhythm, and the art that have reached around the world, opening the hearts and enriching the lives of more than 500 million people in every country, in every language, in every culture. Truly, our world is a happier place because of this perfectly matched and beautifully blended couple, Susan Polis Schutz and Stephen Schutz.

Susan Polis Schutz and Stephen Schutz   Photo by Rocky Thies